Who Invented Basketball?

And Other Questions Kids Have About Sports

by Suzanne Slade   illustrated by Cary Pillo

PICTURE WINDOW BOOKS
a capstone imprint

Special thanks to our advisers for their expertise:

Harry Krampf, Ph.D., Professor of Human Performance
Minnesota State University, Mankato

Terry Flaherty, Ph.D., Professor of English
Minnesota State University, Mankato

Editor: Jill Kalz
Designer: Tracy Davies
Art Director: Nathan Gassman
Production Specialist: Jane Klenk
The illustrations in this book were created with ink and gouache.

Picture Window Books
1710 Roe Crest Drive, North Mankato, Minnesota 56003
www.capstonepub.com

Library of Congress Cataloging-in-Publication Data
Slade, Suzanne.
Who invented basketball? : and other questions kids have about sports /
by Suzanne Slade : illustrated by Cary Pillo.
p. cm.
Includes index.
ISBN 978-1-4048-6049-0 (library binding)
ISBN 978-1-4048-6730-7 (paperback)
1. Sports—Miscellanea—Juvenile literature. 2. Children's questions
and answers. I. Pillo, Cary, ill. II. Title.
GV705.4.S53 2010
796—dc22   2009038201

What are all of the sports?

Jax, age 7

A sport is a physical game that follows certain rules. There are hundreds of different sports. Some sports are played with teams, while others are for just one person. Many sports require special equipment. Some sports are played indoors. Other sports take place on grassy fields, snow-covered hills, or in the water.

Who invented basketball?
Alyssa, age 7

When were basketballs invented?
Samantha, age 8

A teacher named Dr. James Naismith invented basketball in 1891. Back then, players shot soccer balls into peach baskets. The first official basketballs were made of leather. Factories began making basketballs like we use today in 1942.

What is the highest basketball score ever?

Jason, age 8

The highest-scoring National Basketball Association (NBA) game was played on December 13, 1983. The Denver Nuggets played the Detroit Pistons. After three overtimes, the Pistons won. The final score was Pistons 186, Nuggets 184. The total number of points was 370!

Why is soccer so popular outside the United States?

Cruz, age 6

Soccer, called football in many countries, is the most popular sport in the world. It's exciting to play and watch. You don't need much money or equipment to play, either. Since 1996, interest in the sport has grown in the United States. That's the year Major League Soccer began.

What kind of equipment do you need for soccer?

Natalia, age 7

A soccer ball, two goals, and good soccer shoes, called cleats. Players should also wear shin guards and mouthpieces to stay safe.

How many hexagons are on a soccer ball?

Alyssa, age 8

Most soccer balls are made of 20 hexagons (six-sided shapes) and 12 pentagons (five-sided shapes). When sewn together, the 32 pieces make a round ball.

Why can't you touch the ball with your hands in soccer?

Grace, age 7

The game of soccer has 17 laws. Law 12 says players other than the goalie cannot touch the ball with their hands.

When did people start swimming?

Sydney, age 6

People have been swimming across lakes and rivers for thousands of years. In fact, scientists have discovered 6,000-year-old paintings of swimmers from the Stone Age.

Why do you have to take swimming lessons?

Jadyn, age 7

Swimming lessons help you stay safe in water. You can also learn how to swim faster and do different strokes by taking lessons.

How many gold medals did Michael Phelps win in the 2008 Olympics?

Meghan, age 9

Eight! Phelps set a world record for the most gold medals earned at a single Olympics. He earned five medals in individual races and three in relay races.

How many people are on a swimming relay team?

Meghan, age 9

A relay team has four swimmers. Each swimmer takes a turn. The team with the fastest time wins. In a medley relay, each swimmer does a different stroke, such as the butterfly or backstroke.

How many players are on a football team?

Sophie, age 7

How many players are in the NFL?

Brandon, age 8

National Football League (NFL) teams can have no more than 53 active players each. Each team must have 11 players on the field during a game. There are 32 NFL teams, with nearly 1,700 players total.

Who was the first African-American quarterback in the Super Bowl?

Ryan, age 9

Doug Williams was the first African-American quarterback to start in a Super Bowl game. In 1988, Williams completed 18 of 29 passes for the Washington Redskins. He was named the Super Bowl MVP.

Why do football players have numbers on their jerseys?

Izzy, age 8

Numbers make it easy to know who is who. They're much easier to read than names. In 1973, the NFL started giving players numbers based on their position. For example, quarterbacks and kickers have numbers between 1 and 19. Running backs and defensive backs have numbers between 20 and 49.

Is bowling a sport?

Kianna, age 7

Yes, bowling is a sport. Bowlers work with coaches and practice many hours a day. The best bowlers play in tournaments around the world.

How many people are on a bowling team?

Andrea, age 7

A bowling team has two or more people. Four or five is most common. In a bowling league, all teams have the same number of bowlers.

How do people get a strike in bowling?

Draegan, age 6

To get a strike, a bowler knocks down all 10 pins with one ball. It's not easy! Bowlers aim and put just the right spin on the ball. Sometimes a beginning bowler is lucky and gets a strike.

What is the best bowling game?

Saood, age 8

The highest score a bowler can get in one game is 300 points. To get it, a person must roll 12 strikes in a row.

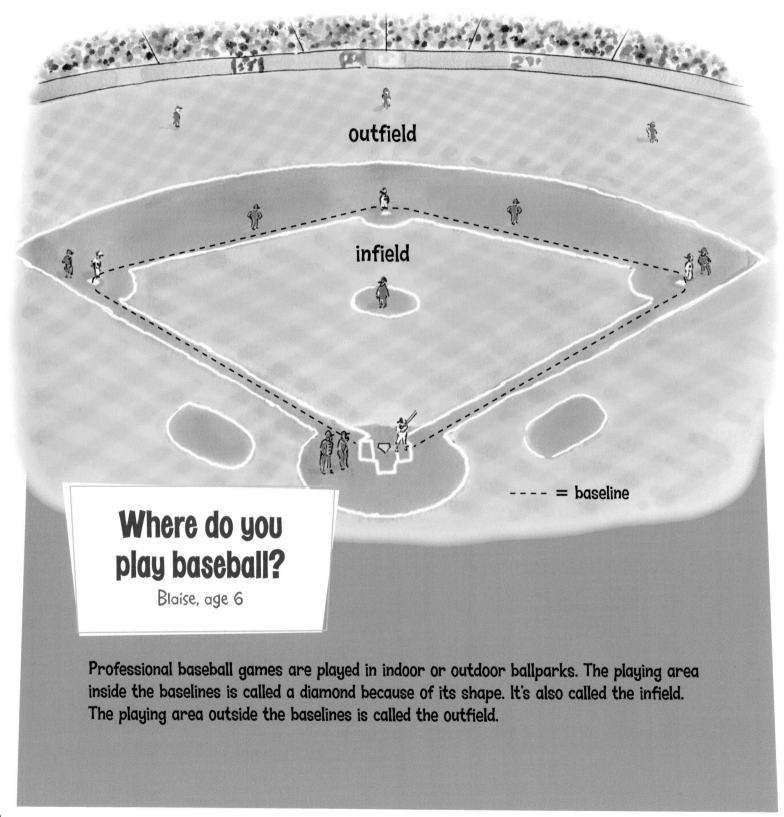

outfield

infield

- - - - = baseline

Where do you play baseball?

Blaise, age 6

Professional baseball games are played in indoor or outdoor ballparks. The playing area inside the baselines is called a diamond because of its shape. It's also called the infield. The playing area outside the baselines is called the outfield.

Why do you have to stay in the white box when you are batting?

James and Logan, age 7

The batter's box is a white rectangle on either side of home plate. Batters stand inside it to make sure everyone is batting from the same spot every time. The batter's box also helps keep swinging bats away from the umpire.

Why is a baseball white with red stitches?

Megan, age 7

A baseball is made of two pieces of white leather. White is easy to see. But no one knows why the cotton stitches are red. The stitches are important. Any bumps on a baseball, such as stitches, affect how the ball flies through the air. Major league baseballs must have exactly 108 stitches.

Who is the fastest runner in the world?

Carissa, age 7

The record holder for the 100-meter dash is usually called the fastest runner in the world. Usain Bolt holds the current record at 9.58 seconds. The Jamaican also holds the world record for the 200-meter: 19.19 seconds.

What do you have to do to run cross-country?

Jadyn, age 7

In the sport of cross-country, people run on trails. The trails may go across fields or through woodlands. Runners even go through water for some races. Men often run longer distances than women.

What are triathlons?

Alex, age 9

A triathlon is a race in which people swim, bike, and run. The person who finishes the race in the shortest time wins. An Ironman triathlon includes a 2.4-mile (3.8-km) swim, 112 miles (179 km) of biking, and ends with a 26.2-mile (42-km) run.

Do you need a special racket to play tennis?

Sophie, age 7

Tennis rackets are specially made for the game of tennis. They have a light outer frame with strings woven inside. The strings are stretched tightly. The center of the racket is called the sweet spot. It's the best spot to hit the tennis ball.

In tennis, what does the word *love* mean?

Jack, age 9

Love means a tennis player has zero points. The word *love* comes from the French word *oeuf*, which means "egg." An egg is shaped like a zero.

Who was the first person to win an official tennis tournament?

Lexi, age 8

In 1877, Spencer Gore won the men's singles title in the first major tennis tournament, called Wimbledon.

What are some sports from countries other than the United States?

Audrey, age 9

People around the world enjoy many sports. Rugby is a rough sport popular in Europe, Japan, Africa, and Australia. It is a bit like football and soccer. Cricket is a bat-and-ball sport played in more than 100 countries. Polo was first played in Asia thousands of years ago. Players try to hit a ball through the other team's goal while on horseback.

cricket

rugby

polo

Who are the best pingpong players in the world?

Freddy, age 8

Pingpong, also called table tennis, became an Olympic sport in 1988. Since then, players from China have won the most medals.

Why do some sports have cheerleaders?

Kate, age 10

Cheerleaders have several jobs at a game. They put on shows for the crowd and get the crowd excited. And they lead the crowd in cheering on the teams. Cheerleaders are most common at football and basketball games.

Why do sports look so easy on TV?

Ethan, age 6

The people playing sports on TV are usually professional athletes. Professional athletes spend a lot of time practicing their skills. They are paid to work out and train. They often do not have other jobs. When athletes do a sport really well, they make that sport look easy.

TO LEARN MORE

More Books to Read

Diehl, David. *Sports A to Z.* New York: Lark Books, 2007.

Hammond, Tim. *Sports.* New York: DK Pub., 2005.

Wyckoff, Edwin Brit. *The Man Who Invented Basketball: James Naismith and His Amazing Game.* Berkeley Heights, N.J.: Enslow Publishers, 2008.

Internet Sites

FactHound offers a safe, fun way to find Internet sites related to this book. All of the sites on FactHound have been researched by our staff.

Here's all you do:

Visit *www.facthound.com*

FactHound will fetch the best sites for you!

GLOSSARY

athlete—a person who plays sports

league—a group of sports teams that play against each other

MVP—short for "most valuable player"

relay—a race between teams in which each team member goes a certain distance and is then replaced by another team member

stroke—a combination of arm and leg movements in swimming

tournament—a contest in which the winner is the one who wins the most games

umpire—a person who makes sure rules are followed in baseball and other sports

INDEX

Look for all of the titles in the Kids' Questions series:

Did Dinosaurs Eat People?
And Other Questions Kids Have About Dinosaurs

Do All Bugs Have Wings?
And Other Questions Kids Have About Bugs

How Do Tornadoes Form?
And Other Questions Kids Have About Weather

What Is the Moon Made Of?
And Other Questions Kids Have About Space

What's Inside a Rattlesnake's Rattle?
And Other Questions Kids Have About Snakes

Who Invented Basketball?
And Other Questions Kids Have About Sports

Why Do Dogs Drool?
And Other Questions Kids Have About Dogs

Why Do My Teeth Fall Out?
And Other Questions Kids Have About the Human Body